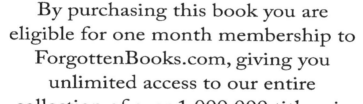

ISBN 978-0-260-61399-8
PIBN 10959649

this
is
our
church

A Presentation of the

First Presbyterian Church,
Main and Roxboro Streets
Durham, N. C.
Organized 1871

Foreword

This booklet is a revised edition of an earlier pamphlet presenting the plant, the program, and the personnel of the First Presbyterian Church, Durham, North Carolina. The Session of the church has authorized the revision and financed its printing.

While retaining the basic structure of the original pamphlet, the committee has changed its form, added certain portions, and brought the information up to date.

This booklet is intended to serve as a friendly introduction to our church for visitors, newcomers and new members; the committee hopes it will also help our members gain an over-all view of the many and varied activities which we call "our church."

The Committee

Our Church

Organized in 1871, the First Presbyterian Church is the oldest Presbyterian church in Durham. With a membership of approximately one thousand, it is the largest Presbyterian church in the city. Despite its age it still enjoys vigorous growth. Despite its size, the individual still stands at the center of its concern. As the "mother of Presbyterianism in Durham County" it has established or helped to establish five other Presbyterian churches. Indicative of its wider concern was a mission station in Korea, built and endowed by the generosity of one of its members of earlier years. Throughout its history, as still today, its spiritual vitality has been manifested by its inclusive program of service seeking to minister to human needs everywhere. It is literally and figuratively true that "the whole city is our parish and the whole world our concern."

Being Presbyterian in faith and order, we are a part of Granville Presbytery, the Synod of North Carolina, and the General Assembly of the Presbyterian Church in the United States. We participate in the total program of our denomination and support all its agencies. Each year more than one third of our budget (provided by the voluntary gifts of our members) goes to benevolences—that is, to the support of the church's ministry and mission beyond the local parish.

Though denominationally loyal, we are not denominationally minded. We are committed to ecumenical (or cooperative) Christianity. That commitment is expressed by our affiliation with the North Carolina Council of Churches, the National Council of the Churches of Christ in America, the World Council of Churches, and the World Alliance of Churches holding the Presbyterian Faith and Government (the last organization being one of the largest Protestant groups in Christendom). It might be said that our first concern is to be Christian, our second concern is to be Protestant, and our third concern is to be Presbyterian. Practically, this has meant that many people with other than Presbyterian background feel fully at home within our fellowship.

The New Testament calls the Church "the Body of Christ in the world." We take that figure of speech seriously, and understand it to mean that Christ is the only rightful Lord and Head of the Church. Consequently we strive to know the mind of Christ, to manifest the spirit of Christ, to obey the will of Christ, and to do the work of Christ and serve His redemptive purpose in and for the world. To that end, we seek to witness by every means at our disposal to the sovereign purpose and love of God, to the salvation from sin that is offered us through Christ our Lord, and to the available presence and power of the Holy Spirit enabling us to live the Christian life. Our aim is to keep our message and our ministry Christ-centered, Biblically sound, theologically mature, socially relevant, and positively and practically helpful in daily living.

Through the years, as at the present time, our membership and constituency have been representative of an inclusive cross-section of the city's life, providing a healthy, stimulating, and enriching fellowship for all. Among the members of First Church can be found people from all walks of life. Most of us are "little people" who never make the headlines. Some are counted "leaders" in the business, commercial, industrial, professional, educational, and civic affairs of the city's life. Within our membership is a large and growing segment of the University community who have found their church home here, and whose presence is a source of encouragement and great usefulness. We have diversity and unity. For this "confederacy of believers" is drawn together and held together by a common loyalty to Christ and a shared purpose to further His Kingdom in the life of the world.

The church plant is composed of three main buildings: the Sanctuary, the Church House, and the Sunday School Building (often called, because of its shape, the Round House). The Sanctuary is air-conditioned, and seats some 600 persons. The Cloister Chapel is part of the Sanctuary building, as are the church office and the offices of the Minister and the Director of Music. Underneath the Sanctuary are attractive and roomy quarters for the Junior High and Senior High Departments.

The Church House is a spacious building with home-like furnishings. It houses the offices of the Director of Christian Education and the Church Hostess, as well as the kitchen and dining facilities. It is the center of week-day activities, and on Sunday provides space for three adult Sunday School classes, two classes of the Kindergarten Department, and the Crib Nursery. It also serves as the center for recreational activities.

The Sunday School Building provides space for the Toddlers, Nursery, Primary, and Junior Departments of the Sunday School.

Adjacent to the church are limited parking facilities and lawn space. Additional and adequate parking facilities are available in the immediate neighborhood of the church.

private and public worship of God is the soul's deliberate and habitual
to the truth and love and purpose of God. Or, as someone has put it,
is keeping the windows of one's life open toward God.'' For that
is the beating heart of the Christian's faith and life. Therefore by
ilable and appropriate means we seek to nourish private devotion and
e inspiring opportunities for corporate or public worship.

services of worship are held each Sunday—the first at 9:45 A.M. (dur-
Sunday School hour), and the second at 11:00 A.M. In an air-
ed sanctuary of simple beauty and dignity the worshiper finds quiet-
physical comfort, emotional peace, mental stimulation, quickening of
ence, spiritual nourishment, and resolution of the will. Our aim is that
ave with renewed strength, recovered courage, and refreshed hope for
hat lie ahead. In the course of a year there are a number of additional
occasional services of worship—such as those that come during the
Easter, Thanksgiving, Advent, and Christmas seasons of the year.

Sacrament of Holy Communion (the Lord's Supper) is celebrated on
ay each quarter at both morning services of worship, and on several
l occasions during the year. As an expression of our particular concern
oung people, their families and friends, there are two special communion
me during the Lenten season, when the members of the Communicants'
officially received into full church membership by the Session; the
e in the early fall, when the young people leave their homes for college
aratory schools.

ours is not just a ''Sunday church,'' we have a mid-week devotional
ch Wednesday at 1:00 P.M. This is open to everyone, but is designed
ly for business people and shoppers. The brief devotional period in
uary is preceded by one luncheon at 12:30 P.M. and followed by
ie at 1:20 P.M.

Cloister Chapel, which has an entrance off Roxboro Street, is open from
to 5:00 P.M. every day of the year. Here the individual may find a
lovely retreat for a brief moment of personal meditation and prayer.
i is also occasionally used for very small weddings and private
services.

Our aim is that no meeting or occasion shall take place in the church buildings without at least a moment of reverence and prayer to express our gratitude to God and to seek His guidance and blessing.

Our Pastoral Ministry

Wherever, whenever, and in whatever the church is involved, the pastor and his assistants are present to lead, to guide, or to support. The pastoral ministry, therefore, includes far more than the Sunday services of worship—or the praying, teaching, and preaching ministry. These, of course, are probably the most important aspects of the minister's total task. In the pulpit he stands before us, the congregation, as our priest, speaking *for us* in his prayers before God; as our teacher, representing the best traditions *of the Church* and of Christian faith and thought as he teaches us and our children; and as our prophet, speaking *for God* in his proclamation of the Word and the administration of the Sacraments.

The minister is well prepared for his preaching and teaching responsibilities through years of training and wide experience. But the ministry is an on-going process, a growing experience. It takes conscientious study, deep thought, and hours of preparation from week to week.

Outside the pulpit, the pastoral ministry widens into an all-encompassing task. It includes visiting in hospitals and homes where there is physical or spiritual need, as well as where there is family joy or some newly awakened interest for God and the church. It brings the pastor into companionship with all of us—in times of happiness as well as in days of sorrow, in the celebrations of the home as well as in sickness and death. It also includes the counseling ministry, the ministry to individuals. All of us are free to come to the minister whenever we need a confidential relationship, understanding, advice, and counsel.

The pastor is also the administrator of the church, the moderator of the Session (the governing body), the chief of the church staff, the originator of most of the church's plans and proposals and programs, the coordinator of the many-sided church activities, the executive who makes decisions and is responsible for the results. He represents our church in the community and in civic organizations. He stands in close relationship to the Presbytery, the Synod,

In a church the size of ours, it is obviously impossible for one ma
demands of such an inclusive task. Our minister, therefore, ha
the Assistant-to-the-Minister, who helps in the pulpit on Sund
takes care of part of the visitation needs during the week; the l
and Church Hostess, who also assumes a share of the visitation
keeping the Church House and its operations running smoothly
taries in the church office, who share the many and varied admi
They all form an effective working team.

E

We start with the proposition that an informed Christian
useful and effective Christian. Therefore we are committed to tl
of Christian education we can fashion from the resources availal
further that Christian education is a continuous process of Cl
spanning the whole of a person's life from birth to death. I
viction our program becomes somewhat like a rowboat that must
two oars. At one oar are the home and the family. At the othe
and its teachers. Thus we think of our educational program a
the final effectiveness of which depends not so much upon the e
curriculum materials and physical equipment as upon how well
fully both oarsmen do their part.

In a sense we regard everything we do here at the church a
educational ministry, designed to contribute something to the ma
ing personalities in the Christian faith and life.

At the hub of our educational program is the Sunday Scl
classes for every age group through senior high school and al

ticularly for adults. Under the able supervision of a trained and experienced Director of Christian Education, and staffed by a large corps of competent and devoted volunteer teachers and workers, our Sunday School has consistently maintained high standards of excellence. All classes meet at 9:45 A.M. each Sunday. In addition, "second-hour sessions" are conducted during the 11:00 A.M. Service of Worship for infants and children up through the Primary Department.

The Sunday School is divided into the following classes and departments:

Children
Crib care nursery.
Toddlers:
   1-year-olds.
   2-year-olds.
   3-year-olds.
Kindergarten:
   4-year-olds.
   5-year-olds.
Primary Department—
   first and second grades.
Primary Department—third grade.
Junior Department—fourth, fifth, and sixth grades.

Young people
Junior High Department—seventh, eighth, and ninth grades.
Senior High Department—tenth, eleventh, and twelfth grades.

Adults
Big Brothers Class—Men's Bible class.
Blacknall Class—Women's Bible class.
Fellowship Class—for men *and* women.

* * *

Clustered around the central hub of the Sunday School are other related groups and activities. On Sunday evenings the Pioneer Youth Fellowship (junior high) and the Senior High Fellowship meet at the Church House at 6:00 P.M. for supper and a program. Here these young people, with the help of adult advisers, develop the qualities of personal Christian leadership by assuming responsibility.

The First Church Forum is a group for young adults which meets at 6:00 P.M. on alternate Sundays for supper and group discussion.

None of the Sunday night groups are limited to our own congregation, but all interested persons are sincerely welcomed.

In cooperation with the local YMCA, the church sponsors basketball and softball teams for boys and men.

During the Lenten season each year the minister conducts a Communicants' Class for young people preparing for church membership. At meetings held every Saturday morning for six to eight weeks the minister seeks to interpret the essential elements of the Christian faith and life in terms that are understandable and meaningful to a young person.

During the summer months many recreational and spiritually enriching activities are carried on by the church:

Vacation Church School is a carefully planned one-week program conducted for children through the sixth grade. In addition to its educational and recreational program, instruction in choral singing is given by the Director of Music.

Some time during August members of all the Presbyterian Youth Fellowships in Durham hold a Youth Activities Week, meeting nightly at one of the churches for supper, an inspirational talk, discussions in small groups divided according to age, and a program of recreation.

As a member of Granville Presbytery, our church participates in the excellent year-round program at our new camp and conference grounds, Presbyterian Point, situated on Kerr Lake. The camping programs in the summer are particularly appealing to the children and young people.

The various conferences held at Montreat in the summer for both young people and adults are always richly satisfying religious experiences for those who attend.

- - *

For the adult members of the congregation definite annual programs are planned to provide education and inspiration.

The Durham Presbyterian School of Christian Growth is a cooperative effort of all the Presbyterian churches in Durham. This meets on five successive nights, and persons registering for the school have a choice of three or four study courses in which to enroll.

Usually in the fall and again during the Lenten season a special series of Bible study lectures, taught by a qualified theologian, are given on five or six successive Wednesday nights.

All Sunday School teachers participate in the Workers Conference, which meets every other month for dinner. The program following the meal is designed to strengthen and enrich the entire Sunday School program. In addition, individual departmental meetings are called as often as necessary.

Since the home and family are an indispensable part of our educational "team effort," we not only seek the parents' understanding and cooperation in what we are trying to do at the church; we also endeavor to put into their hands every helpful tool that will enable them to do their part. Pamphlets and literature are provided for use in the home, and parents and teachers are encouraged to meet together on departmental "family nights" and other occasions.

The organization known as the Women of the Church is an active and integral part of our total church program. Its object is to unite in Christian fellowship all the women of our church, and to provide opportunities for them to study and apply the teachings of Christ in all areas of life. Its goal is to enlist in training and in service all the women in our church. To accomplish this goal, varied and well organized groups meet at monthly intervals.

On the first Monday of each month the various circles meet in small, intimate groups, usually in the homes of the members. The circles follow a fairly well defined program: a period of simple refreshments and fellowship, followed by a business meeting for discussion of circle projects and the work of the various agencies of the church, and a Bible study. The Bible study takes the form of a discussion drawing in all members of the group, and has proved to be a real meeting of minds in an effort to apply the principles of Christ to all areas of life.

While most of the circles meet in the morning, there are also groups which meet on the first Monday night of each month, and a business women's circle which meets for supper on the second Tuesday of the month.

On the second Monday of each month the group meets as a whole for a program designed to educate our women in the total program of the Presbyterian Church. This follows fairly closely the excellent material available through our Board of Women's Work, which stresses world-wide Christian missions, church extension, General Fund agencies, and so forth. Our aim is to promote the spiritual, educational, social, and financial welfare of the church and to encourage the women to bear personal witness to Christ.

Our Ministry of Music

Music is the heart's native language. From earliest Biblical times it has been associated with the adoration and praise of God. It holds an important place in our church. Believing that a knowledge and love of sacred music is a part of a Christian's rightful heritage, we have recently strengthened this aspect of our ministry. Under the leadership of a trained, competent, and full-time Organist and Director of Music, with the excellent help of a part-time assistant, we now have seven organized choirs, with further expansion planned. When a child reaches the age of 4, he or she may enroll in the Children's Choir and begin an enriching experience of learning and singing good music. As the children grow older and more experienced, they move upward through the various choirs. The older children sing in the services of worship on several occasions during the year, and participate in the program of Christmas music. The Carillon Choir—Durham's first bell choir—is made up of boys in the seventh grade and beyond.

At present the choirs are set up as follows:

Children's Choir—4- and 5-year-olds.
Carol Choir—boys and girls in the first, second, and third grades.
Crusader Choir—boys and girls in the fourth, fifth, and sixth grades.
Carolette Choir—girls in the seventh and eighth grades.
Chapel Choir—boys and girls from the ninth through the twelfth grade.
Chancel Choir—the adult choir.
Carillon Choir (a special choir of bells)—boys from the seventh grade up.

Altogether some 160 persons are participating in the music program of the church, all on a volunteer basis. Rehearsal days are changed periodically to accommodate the members. All parts of our music program are closely related to our educational program, and each enriches the other.

Our Ministry of Fellowship

Fellowship, as we normally think of the term, is not so much a studied aim of the church's ministry as it is one of the many by-products that result when Christian people live, learn, work, and worship together in the church. It is somewhat like the fragrance that hovers over a rose garden in full bloom: Fellowship is not the bush or the bloom; it is the pleasant fragrance. There are occasions, of course—such as our coffee hours, play nights, parties, dances, and other recreational activities—when our immediate purpose is simply to get better acquainted and to enjoy one another's company, for the sheer joy that comes from such association. Most of the time, however, our sense of fellowship is a kind of constant overtone that accompanies all that we do. While the main purpose of our many organizations and activities is learning, serving, and witnessing, yet the enriching by-product in all is this feeling of oneness, "at-homeness," and friendliness that comes from being together, learning together, and serving together in worth-while endeavors. Our aim is that no one shall feel like a stranger in our midst, and that none shall feel left out or alone. Our comradeship with Christ brings us a comradeship with one another. We believe that here at First Church everyone can find this same sense of Christian fellowship which those of us who have been here longer have found good, satisfying, and rewarding.

To further implement and strengthen our ministry of fellowship, and as an evidence of our Christian concern for persons inside and outside the church, the Parish Plan was organized some time ago. For this purpose the city has been divided into a number of smaller "parishes," each with 12 to 20 church families, and each having a family designated as "parish leaders."

The purpose of the Parish Plan is twofold.

1. In a large downtown church, with two worship services, it is difficult for the members to get acquainted and to feel the warmth and unity of the church fellowship. Through the closer fellowship of the individual parishes, it is hoped that a deeper sense of belonging will be fostered among us.

2. Within a large membership like ours there is always a great need for visitation and information concerning special needs. We also have a large potential of active members to visit and pass information on. The new plan was devised to encourage all church members to feel a responsibility for visiting in their parishes and informing the church office about special visitation needs: newcomers to town, prospective members, homebound members, and hospitalized members. The Parish Plan should also help to make new members feel more welcome, and make it possible for us to maintain closer contact with inactive and "retired roll" members.

Another very practical means of tying our membership closer together in fellowship, understanding, and love is the newssheet, entitled *Koinonos* (from the Greek word meaning partner, associate, companion, or sharer). This "newsy" bulletin, which is mailed to the entire membership, carries many items of interest and announcements not printed in the more formal church bulletin.

Both the church bulletin and *Koinonos* are mailed to students in colleges a
preparatory schools, and to all our homebound members.

The Church Fellowship (for all adult members of the church) meets month
for dinner and a program. While the principal purpose of this group is to p
vide an informal setting in which old and new members alike may becon
better acquainted, the meetings are planned to stimulate Christian thinking
well as to foster Christian fellowship.

Ou
Ministr
c
Servic

The ideal and the motivation for Christian service are inherent in 1
Biblical teaching of "the stewardship of all of life." The meaning of this phr;
s that all we are and all we have comes finally from the love and mercy of G
and from our membership in human society. We are dependent and int
dependent creatures; no one is really self-sufficient, for we need each oth
God's final judgment upon every man's life is, "What have you done with wl
you have?"

Believing that we live under the obligation to put back into life somethi
for all that we receive, we seek to train and equip our members for constructi
service, to cultivate in them the desire to serve, and then to provide opportunit
for that service. We do not assume that the Christian's proper service is cc
fined to what he does within the church. We believe that Christian service mu
also reach out into the life of the community. Therefore you will find our me
bers actively participating—sometimes far out of proportion to our numeric
strength—in every worth-while community endeavor. At the same time, ho
ever, we believe that a church member should give high priority to the nee
and the calls of the church for a fair portion of his time, his talents, and l
possessions.

The doors of our church are open seven days a week, and the doors of o
ministry of service are never closed. No human need knocking at these do
is irrelevant to us, and no human problem is too small to claim our attenti
Within the limitations of our ability, we seek to carry on a ministry of serv

as wide as the dimensions of human need and as inclusive as the expanse of human concern. Through visitation and pastoral care, personal counseling, and sympathetic friendship, we seek to release the healing and helping forces of Christian love and good will whenever and wherever we can. Through a limited program of social action we seek to fill the immediate needs of persons who ask our help and support. And through the mission, church extension, and benevolence agencies of our church—in preaching, teaching, and healing—we extend this ministry of service throughout the world.

Our Invitation to You

We have tried to tell you a bit about our church, about our understanding of the meaning and the implications of the Christian faith and the Christian life, and about what we are trying to be and do here at First Church. We hope you have found it interesting and informative.

We believe that every sincere and serious-purposed person who wishes to commit himself or herself to the Christian faith and the Christian life can find somewhere close at hand a church fellowship that is congenial and helpful to his or her spiritual needs and aspirations, and one that offers ample opportunity for growth and service.

Under that conviction we invite you to come and visit us, to learn more about us, and to give us the pleasure and privilege of knowing you better. Should you find here, as many have, what you want as a "church home" for yourself and your family, then, in the name of Christ and with all the sincerity and friendliness at our command, we would welcome you into the life and ministry of the First Presbyterian Church. Our invitation is simple, genuine, and forthright. We shall not harass or annoy you about "joining our church." We want you to know that whenever you are ready the doors to this church and to our Christian fellowship are open and waiting to welcome you. Should you wish to talk further about this matter, you need only to call the church office, or speak to any officer or member of the church. Your request will be passed on to the minister.

Our invitation to you may be summed up in this word from the Bible: "Come with us and we will seek to do thee good." We are also confident that **you** can do us great good.

How Does
One Join
the Presbyterian Church?

In the Presbyterian church the Session (the governing body) admits persons to membership. After being received by the Session, new members are later (usually at the next communion service) welcomed by the congregation and given their certificates of membership and other literature concerning the church. Almost every Sunday the invitation to membership is given from the pulpit. The Session meets in the Cloister Chapel following the close of the 11:00 A.M. Service of Worship, and new members may be received at that time.

Persons who have never been members of any church join by *profession of faith*. This may be a simple statement about your personal religious faith, or it may be affirmative answers to certain questions concerning your faith in and commitment to Christ as Lord and Saviour. Persons who have never been baptized receive the sacrament of baptism—a simple rite symbolizing their entrance into the church.

Persons who have been members of other Protestant churches may be received by *Letter of Transfer*. We will write to the church of your former membership and request such transfer.

When for any reason (such as loss of church records) such Letters of Transfer are not available, a person may be received by *re-affirmation of faith*. This again may be your own statement of your desire to become a member of this church, or your affirmative answers to certain simple questions along the same line.

For temporary residents of Durham (undergraduate and graduate students, nurses, interns, instructors, and any others here for a short while) who desire an active relationship with a local church without severing membership with their home church *affiliate* membership is available. Affiliate membership offers all the privileges and responsibilities of regular membership except voting and election to the Session and Diaconate.

Schedule of Sunday Services

9:45 A.M.—Sunday School, with classes for all ages and nurseries for infants.

9:45 A.M.—First Service of Worship.

10:45 A.M.—Second-hour Sunday School session for babies and children through the Primary Department.

11:00 A.M.—Second Service of Worship.

6:00 P.M.—Supper for the Pioneer Youth Fellowship and the Senior High Fellowship.

6:30 P.M.—Meetings and programs for the Pioneer Youth Fellowship and the Senior High Fellowship.

Each Sunday's bulletin carries a calendar of regular and special events for the following week.

ries for infants.

hildren through

the Senior High

owship and the

ecial events for

Mrs Harret Morgan
1411 Anderson St
Oakland
72

OUR CHURCH

FOREWORD

The Steering Committee appreciates the cooperation of the many members who aided in the preparation of this brochure. We especially thank Mrs. Howard Gamble for her pictorial supervision; Whitley & Scott, photographers; Seeman Printery; and George Watts Fowler, art director, Harvey-Massengale Co.

We regret the omission of many children in the class photographs which were taken during the peak of the mcasels epidemic.

OUR CHURCH

OUR CHURCH

"Early in the Spring of 1876, as soon as roof, weatherboarding and floor were in place, we began to worship in our little sanctuary. . . . Planks laid across boxes served as seats. A fruit crate with a piano cover spread over it furnished a pulpit. . . . Each family carried a lamp from home on preaching nights to light the church."

Thus, is written the History of The First Presbyterian Church of Durham in description of our first church building.

Humble? According to today's standards, yes. But to our courageous forefathers it represented a dream accomplished. And to pay for that dream they reached into both their savings and their precious credit. But

Nursery Department

Kindergarten Department

porary haven until they could have a place of their very own in which to worship. When organized the Church had 11 members. By 1877—six years later—there were 36 members, eighteen enrolled in Sunday School with six teachers.

Primary Department—First Grade

Primary Department—Third Grade

Junior Department—Fourth Grade

Junior Department—Sixth Grade

Seventh Grade Girls

Seventh Grade Boys

ghth and Ninth Grade Boys

:h and Ninth Grade Girls

Senior High School Class

College Students

Young Adults

Blacknall Bible Class

and his family was still further evidenced in 1922 with their gift of the Church House. School and to its training of our children and young people in particular.

Big Brothers Bible Class

The Women of the Church

had come for action to meet the needs of our Sunday School. World War II years not only made this impossible but also added to the problem as fresh generations in unprecedented number were added to the roll.

Strange not then was it that in the minds of the congregation at large the need for point up the necessity for additional facilities.

This need was spelled out by an investigating committee's report of 1948-49 on School needs. Chief findings are described on the following two pages. Clearly, the Sunday School of The First Presbyterian Church of

Religious Education Teachers

1913—Adequate Facilities   1949—Crowded, Outmoded

Durham is at a cross-road. We either press onward or we close our eyes to our responsibilities to our children. Simultaneously, needs of the Church's choir and of the kitchen were studied. They, too, are summarized on the following pages . . . and the story is the same. The situation is critical. Rightfully proud as we are of our past, we cannot any

In 1913 when our Sunday School Building was erected, adequate space and facilities became available. Today we are trying to serve twice as many children in the same space with practically the same equipment. Not a single major capital expenditure has been made on our Sunday School needs for

- Some classes do not have a room of their own

adopted fully because equipment is either lacking or antiquated.

(For a detailed account, class by class, read "Survey of Need for Our Present and Immediately Anticipated Sunday School Program.")

organist in close touch with the choir. This. The young people will probably furnish the nucleus
can be done by moving forward the balcony of your choir a few years hence. As the situa-
and choir and the pulpit and platform now exists virtually closing the
As shown by the architect's drawings, the door in their infancy. Our committee feels
improvements can be made gracefully most emphatically that relief should be given
Your particular attention is directed to the enlarging choir loft along the lines
follow excerpt from Music Music indicated."

KITCHEN

class and realize how pressing is the need for attractive, additional space and facilities. All of us may not have talented sons and daughters who would like to sing in the Church Choir if there were room for them. Only a limited number of us understand the technicalities of heating, plumbing, construction and how needed are repairs and replacements in this department of our Church property. But the kitchen, that's different. We have only to take one look at the kitchen in the Church House and compare it with the kitchen in our own home to realize that the Survey Committee did·not exaggerate in its harsh description.

While members of most every other church have answered repeated calls, we have not been asked to contribute other than operating expenses for our Church and Sunday School property in almost 35 years!

The goal is $125,000. That is what is needed to get improved and new Sunday School facilities, enlarged choir loft, and a modern kitchen. By far the largest share of the monies needed is for the Sunday School, a phase of our Church particularly close to the spiritual life of our children. We cannot, we will not fail them.

us have had to dig deep in the past for our Church, we may have become soft givers. Frankly, your Committee is aware of this danger but is equally confident that each and every one of us will regard the challenge of this campaign seriously and sincerely, and give accordingly.

If we do, the goal will be OVER-SUB-SCRIBED THE FIRST YEAR! Indeed, this financial drive can become a fresh, invigorating force resulting in renewed membership interest and rededication of loyalty. In that spirit you are invited to share in this vital enterprise.

(Signed) C. A. Croft, *Chairman, Session's Executive Committee;* Charles S. Sydnor, Sr., *Clerk of Session;* Robert S. Hays, Jr., *Chairman, Board of Deacons;* W. W. Couch, Jr., *Chairman, Steering Committee;* Mrs. Wm. M. Coppridge, Carl R. Harris, John L. Moorhead, Howard W. Gamble, William Muirhead, J. F. Wily, Jr., *Steering Committee members.*

Carr, Mrs. Albert G.
Carr, Charles H.
Carr, Miss June
Carr, Mrs. J. W., Jr.
Carr, Mrs. Mamie L.
Carr, William A.
Carr, Mrs. W. F.
Carr, W. F., Jr.
Cates, Mrs. Bertha L.
Cates, Samuel Olive
Causey, Mrs. A. B.
Causey, Odell C.
Chamberlain, J. W.
Champion, Mrs. Wm. C.
Chase, Rodney Y.
Chase, Mrs. Rodney Y.
Christian, Harry L.
Christian, Mrs. Harry L.
Christian, John W.
Christian, Mrs. John W.
Christian, Miss Mary Anne
Christian, John W., Jr.
Clark, Mrs. W. H.
Clifton, Miss Julia
Cobb, Mrs. Alphonsus
Cobb, Rawls
Cobb, J. B.
Cobb, Mrs. James O.
Cobb, James O., Jr.
Cobb, Paul Whitlock
Cobb, Miss Virginia
Cole, E. Duncan
Cole, Mrs. E. Duncan
Coleman, H. G.
Coleman, Mrs. H. G.
Coley, Mrs. Eva Pruitt
Collins, Miss Annie Haines
Conant, Dr. Norman F.
Conant, Mrs. Norman F.
Conant, Norman F., Jr.
Conant, Miss Sylvia
Conant, Miss Linda
Cooke, Mrs. Walter D.
Coonradt, Mr. Raphael W.
Coppridge, Dr. Wm. M.
Coppridge, Mrs. Wm. M.
Coppridge, Jimmy
Coston, J. A.
Coston, Mrs. J. A.
Couch, W. W., Jr.
Couch, Mrs. W. W., Jr.
Couch, Miss Elizabeth
Covington, Wm. R.
Covington, Mrs. Wm. R.
Crabill, W. C.
Crabill, Mrs. W. C.
Craig, C. M.
Craig, Mrs. C. M.
Craig, Major C. M.
Crawford, Miss Clara
Creadick, Dr. Robert N.
Creadick, Mrs. Robert N.
Crenshaw, Roy N.
Crenshaw, Mrs. Roy N.
Croft, C. A.
Croft, Mrs. C. A.
Croft, Mrs. I. C.
Croom, Wm. D.
Croom, Mrs. Wm. D.
Crotts, Mrs. M. L.
Crowder, Mrs. F. W.
Crumpler, Miss Berta
Currie, Claude
Damon, Mrs. W. E.
Daniel, S. V.
Daniel, Mrs. S. V.
Daniel, S. V., Jr.

Dukes, Charles A.
Dukes, Mrs. Charles A.
Dukes, Charles A., Jr.
Dunn, G. Thomas
Dunn, Mrs. G. Thomas
Dunn, Richard Lee
Dunn, Earl
Dunn, L. L.
Dunn, Lucian
Eason, Miss Martha
Edmonds, Eugene
Edwards, Mrs. Polly
Edwards, Mrs. W. P.
Elliott, Benjamin W.
Elliott, Mrs. Benjamin W.
Elliott, Benjamin W., Jr.
Elliott, Mrs. Benjamin W., Jr.
Elliott, Robert Day
Elliott, Mrs. Robert Day
Englund, Mrs. Gosta
Enoch, J. Robert
Enoch, Mrs. J. Robert
Epperson, Dr. J. H.
Epperson, Mrs. J. H.
Epperson, Wm. T.
Epperson, Mrs. Wm. T.
Erexson, Mrs. Sarah W.
Everett, Dr. John W.
Everett, Mrs. John W.
Everett, Ronald Wilcox
Everett, Mrs. R. O.
Everett, Robinson O.
Ferguson, A. L.
Ferguson, Mrs. A. L.
Ferguson, Miss Ruth
Fleming, Archie
Fleming, Mrs. Archie
Forbus, Elizabeth T.
Forbus, Sample B.
Forbus, Mrs. Sample B.
Franck, Mrs. W. F.
Fuller, Mrs. R. B.
Fuquay, Mrs. Mary K.
Fuquay, Harold H.
Fuquay, Robert E.
Gallyon, Mrs. Sadie S.
Gamble, Howard W.
Gamble, Mrs. Howard W.
Gamble, Miss Tonya
Gardner, Dr. Clarence E., Jr.
Gardner, Mrs. Clarence E., Jr.
Gardner, Jane Lockwood
Garrard, Mrs. D. L.
Gattis, Lee Roy
Gattis, Mrs. Lee Roy
Gibson, George W.
Gibson, Mrs. George W.
Gibson, James R.
Gibson, John H.
Gifford, Mrs. Henry
Girvin, Davidson K.
Girvin, Mrs. Davidson K.
Glymph, Grover C.
Glymph, Mrs. Grover C.
Glymph, Grover C., Jr.
Glymph, H. Kelly
Goodwin, Lee C.
Goodwin, Mrs. Lee C.
Goodwin, Miss Noma Lee
Graham, Neil A.
Graham, Mrs. Neil A.
Graham, Ralph Leach
Graham, Neil A., Jr.
Graham, Mrs. John B.
Gray, Mrs. Irving
Green, Mrs. Ida R.
Green, Mrs. W. M.

Hager, Mrs. Virgil D.
Hager, Miss Nancy Ann
Hager, John Henry
Hagerty, Barton G.
Hagerty, Mrs. Barton G.
Hall, John R. (Affiliate)
Hall, Mrs. W. H.
Hamblen, Mrs. E. C.
Hamblen, Miss Agnes
Hammett, Mrs. F. M.
Hammett, Miss Bessie
Hammett, Miss Sallie
Happer, Mrs. William W., Jr.
Harden, Milton R.
Harden, Mrs. Milton R.
Harper, Mrs. R. W.
Harris, Carl R.
Harris, Mrs. Carl R.
Harris, Miss Nancy E.
Harris, Thomas Cooper Hicks
Harris, Luttie T.
Harris, Mrs. Mary Cobb
Harris, W. Page, Jr.
Harris, Ransom S., Jr.
Harris, Mrs. W. I.
Hay, Thomas T.
Hay, Mrs. Thomas T.
Haynes, Charles C., Jr.
Haynes, Mrs. Charles C., Jr.
Hays, Robert S., Jr.
Hays, Mrs. Robert S., Jr.
Hays, Miss Laura
Hays, Robert S., III
Heady, Mrs. Raymond A.
Heflin, Frances Gibbs
Hendrickson, Horace J.
Hendrickson, Mrs. Horace J.
Hendrix, Dr. James P.
Hendrix, Mrs. James P.
Hicks, C. Spears
Hicks, Mrs. C. Spears
High, Mrs. Herman
Hill, George Watts
Hill, Mrs. Kate F.
Hill, Thomas Fuller
Hill, Mrs. Thomas Fuller
Hill, Thomas Fuller, Jr.
Hill, J. F.
Hill, Mrs. J. F.
Hill, John Sprunt
Hill, T. C.
Hill, Mrs. T. C.
Hills, Fred H.
Hills, Mrs. Fred H.
Hinshaw, W. B.
Hinshaw, Mrs. W. B.
Hobbs, Mrs. William T.
Holeman, Miss Hallie
Holeman, Miss Jean
Holeman, Richard B., Jr.
Hollingshead Miss Betty Layne
Holt, I. T. (Jack)
Holt, Mrs. I. T.
Honeycutt, Wm. A.
Honeycutt, Mrs. Wm. A.
Honeycutt, Wm. D.
Hooker, Mrs. C. E.
Hooker, Miss Lela
Huckabee, Mrs. J. D.
Huffer, Charles O.
Huffer, Mrs. Charles O.
Hughes, John Knox
Hughes, Mrs. John Knox
Hughes, Samuel Morton
Hundley, J. Camden
Hundley, Mrs. J. Camden

Irvine, Mrs. J. Elliott
Isenhour, V. O., Jr.
Jeffreys, Mrs. W. B.
Jeffreys, Frances Civilla
Jones, Charles F.
Jones, Mrs. Charles F.
Jones, E. Leyburn
Jones, Miss Eliza
Jones, Ralph G.
Jones, Mrs. T. J.
Jones, Miss Margaret
Jones, Thomas J., Jr.
Jones, Mrs. Thomas J., Jr.
Jones, Dr. Thomas T.
Jones, Mrs. Thomas T.
Jones, David Randolph
Jordan, A. C.
Jordan, Mrs. A. C.
Karriker, Mrs. Thurman R.
Keith, Mrs. Hudie C.
Keir, Henry B.
Keir, Mrs. Henry B.
Kelley, Douglas L.
Kelley, Mrs. Douglas L.
Kelly, Thomas L.
Kelly, Mrs. Thomas L.
Kemp, Mrs. N. P.
Kemp, Miss Virginia
Kennedy, Mrs. John
Kerns, Dr. Thomas C.
Kerns, Mrs. Thomas C.
Kerns, Thomas C., Jr.
Kerns, Mrs. Thomas C., Jr.
Kerr, John T., Jr.
Kerr, Mrs. John T., Jr.
Kerr, John T., III
King, E. E.
King, Mrs. E. E.
Knight, E. F.
Knight, Mrs. E. F.
Korstian, Dr. C. F.
Korstian, Mrs. C. F.
Korstian, Miss Grace
Lanning, Mrs. Edna E.
Leary, Dr. Lewis, Jr.
Leary, Mrs. Lewis, Jr.
Leathers, John B.
Leathers, Mrs. John B.
Leathers, Wm. A.
Leathers, Mrs. Wm. A.
Lee, J. Grover
Lee, Mrs. J. Grover
Lee, J. Grover, Jr.
Lee, Thomas Howerton
Lewis, P. C.
Lewis, Mrs. P. C.
Lewis, Phillip A.
Ligon, Mrs. Joel A.
Ligon, James Wendell
Lindsey, Miss Dorothy Melba
Lipscomb, Mrs. J. M.
Lipscomb, J. M., Jr.
Lloyd, Mrs. Flora V.
Long, Mrs. Jack
Lyon, Mrs. Joe T.
Lyon, Joe T., Jr.
MacCaughelty, Mrs. Thomas
MacKinnon, Oliver P.
MacKinnon, Mrs. Oliver P.
MacMillan, John D.
Mangum, Mrs. J. Pender
Mann, L. C.
Mann, Mrs. L. C.
Marlette, Nelda Frances
Martin, Mrs. John Wade
Mason, Mrs. J. B.
Mason, Charles M.
Matthews, C. S.

Matthews, Mrs. C. S.
Matthews, L. T.
Matthews, Mrs. L. T.
Matthews, Lonnie T., Jr.
Matthis, Mrs. George M.
Maughan, Mrs. William Fairfield
Maughan, Miss Barbara Fairfield
Maughan, Miss Mary Margot
Michie, Mrs. J. C.
Michie, William P.
Milam, R. S.
Milam, Mrs. R. S.
Milam, James P.
Miller, E. M.
Miller, Mrs. E. M.
Miller, John K.
Miller, Mrs. John K.
Miller, L. P.
Miller, Mrs. L. P.
Minter, Wm. D.
Minter, Mrs. Wm. D.
Montgomery, Miss Mary Frances
Montgomery, R. G.
Montgomery, Mrs. R. G.
Montsinger, H. E.
Montsinger, Mrs. H. E.
Montsinger, Homer E., Jr.
Moody, Mrs. Clarice Pleasants
Moorhead, John Lynne
Moorhead, Mrs. John Lynne
Morehead, J. Lathrop
Morehead, Mrs. J. Lathrop
Morgan, Mrs. Amarantha Ray
Morgan, Mrs. W. L.
Morgan, Willard B.
Muirhend, William
Muirhead, Mrs. William
Muirhead, Alastair
Murray, Mrs. E. C.
Murray, W. G.
Murray, Mrs. W. G.
Murray, Miss Clara
Murray, Mrs. W. R.
Myers, Mrs. Ida
McCaskill, J. M.
McCue, J. Cameron
McCue, Mrs. J. Cameron
McDermott, Dr. Malcolm
McDermott, Mrs. Malcolm
McDermott, Malcolm, Jr.
McDevett, Wm. S.
McDevett, Mrs. Wm. S.
McDevett, Jo Anne
McDonald, D. L.
McDonald, Mrs. D. L.
McDonald, Mrs. L. C.
McGarvey, Miss Marie L.
McGranaham, Mrs. Anna
McGranaham, Mrs. L. N.
McIver, Mrs. Evan G.
McIver, Evan G., Jr.
McIver, Mrs. Evan G., Jr.
McKee, Mrs. Ada
McNutt, James M.
McNutt, Mrs. James M.
McPherson, Dr. S. D.
McPherson, Mrs. S. D.
McPherson, Dr. Sam D., Jr.
McPherson, Mrs. S. D., Jr.
Neathery, W. M.

Neely, Mrs. W. J.
Newton, Walter C.
Newton, Mrs. Walter C.
Newton, Miss Betty
Newton, Walter Cheek
Niblock, Miss Jamie
Nisbet, Miss Mary G.
Noblin, W. W.
Noblin, Mrs. W. W.
Norris, Paul W.
Norris, Mrs. Paul W.
O'Briant, Mrs. Hubert
O'Briant, Mrs. John A.
O'Briant, Mrs. M. S.
Odom, James A.
Odom, Mrs. James A.
Odom, James A., Jr.
Odom, Richard
Odom, Terrance
O'Kelley, Mrs. J. M.
Oldham, Mrs. L. B.
Oosting, Dr. Henry J.
Oosting, Mrs. Henry J.
Owen, Fred C.
Owen, Mrs. Fred C.
Owen, Miss Elizabeth
Patterson, Lyndon C.
Patterson, Robert D.
Patton, James R., Jr.
Patton, Mrs. James R., Jr.
Patton, James R., III
Patton, Macon Glasgow
Paulsen, Miss Gladys
Pearse, Dr. Richard L.
Pearse, Mrs. Richard L.
Peeler, James Lee
Peeler, Mrs. James Lee
Peeler, Jonathan Lee
Peeler, Miss Claudia
Penn, Mrs. H. L.
Penn, Miss Margaret Lee
Perry, Curtis
Perry, Mrs. J. D.
Perry, Mrs. Nathaniel
Pickett, Sycho
Pickett, Mrs. Sycho
Pleasants, J. L.
Plowden, Miss Mary E.
Poole, Robert F., Jr.
Poole, Mrs. Robert F., Jr.
Pope, Marvin H.
Pope, Mrs. Marvin H.
Porter, A. K.
Porter, Frederick A.
Porter, Joseph E.
Porter, Mrs. Joseph E.
Pounds, J. C., Jr.
Powell, Dr. Albert H.
Powell, Mrs. Albert H.
Powell, Albert H., Jr.
Powell, Wm. Douglas
Pratt, Lanier W.
Pratt, Mrs. Lanier W.
Preston, Dr. Rhea S.
Preston, Mrs. Rhea S.
Proctor, W. L.
Proctor, Mrs. W. L.
Raney, Mrs. R. B.
Rankin, Dr. Robert S.
Rankin, Mrs. Robert S.
Ray, J. Marvin
Ray, Mrs. J. Marvin

Reese, Mrs. Riley B.
Reese, Miss Sarah Anne
Regen, Mrs. Kelsey
Regen, Jon
Regen, Miss Margot
Reinhart, Henry P.
Reinhart, Mrs. Henry P.
Reynolds, Dr. Gordon W.
Reynolds, Mrs. Gordon W.
Rich, Miss Anna
Ricketson, Dr. R. A. Greer
Riggs, Mrs. J. B.
Robb, Joseph A., Jr.
Robb, Mrs. Joseph A., Jr.
Roberson, Dr. Foy
Roberson, Mrs. Foy
Roberson, Miss Helen
Robert, Dr. Joseph C.
Robert, Mrs. Joseph C.
Robert, Frank C.
Roberts, Dr. Louis C.
Roberts, Mrs. Louis C.
Robertson, M. D.
Robertson, Mrs. M. D.
Robertson, Marion D., Jr.
Robins, James Adkins III
Robinson, W. L.
Robinson, Mrs. W. L.
Rochelle, Z. A.
Rochelle, Mrs. Z. A.
Rogers, Miss Betty Cheek
Rollins, Mrs. Steed
Rose, Mrs. Hewitt
Ross, Mrs. Harvey P.
Ross, Dr. Robert A.
Ross, Mrs. Robert A.
Sasser, L. L.
Scanlon, Mrs. David H.
Scanlon, David H., Jr.
Scanlon, Mrs. David H., Jr.
Scarlett, Mrs. E. H.
Schneider, Mrs. Walter
Separk, Mrs. W. D.
Separk, W. D., Jr.
Shackelford, Mrs. E. W.
Shackelford, Walter E.
Shackelford, Daniel O.
Shaw, Clyde Alexander, Jr.
Simpson, Walter L.
Simpson, Mrs. Walter L.
Simpson, Natalie
Simpson, Dr. William H.
Simpson, Mrs. William H.
Simpson, Mrs. William L.
Sisk, Mrs. Harold
Skillen, Mrs. James Randall
Skinner, Charles R.
Skinner, Mrs. Charles R.
Smith, Mrs. Albert N.
Smith, Dr. Annie T.
Smith, Walter Gold
Spain, Mrs. W. L.
Spencer, Mrs. John A.
Spicer, Gordon M.
Stanford, Dr. W. Raney
Stanford, Stephen D.
Stansbury, Dale F.
Stansbury, Mrs. Dale F.
Stansbury, Miss Patricia Ann
Stansbury, Miss Betty Stuart
Stevenson, Mrs. A. H.
Still, John T.
Still, Mrs. John T.

Stinespring, Mrs. W. F.
Stinespring, William Forrest
Stinespring, John
Stocker, Dr. Frederick W.
Stocker, Mrs. Frederick W.
Stocker, Miss Maya Maria
Stocker, Miss Gabrielle
Stocker, Miss Evelyn E.
Stow, Mrs. G. A.
Strayhorn, A. R.
Strayhorn, Mrs. Ralph N.
Strayhorn, Ralph N., Jr.
Stuart, Mrs. Charles E.
Sydnor, Dr. Charles S.
Sydnor, Mrs. Charles S.
Sydnor, Charles S., Jr.
Sydnor, Victor
Taylor, Mrs. A. B.
Taylor, Mrs. Jack A.
Teasley, Mrs. B. F.
Thiele, Miss Marguerite Albert
Tilley, Mrs. Donald L.
Tilley, Mrs. Eric L., Jr.
Tisdale, Mrs. J. R.
Toms, Mrs. C. W., Jr.
Totten, W. H.
Trevathan, J. L.
Trevathan, Mrs. J. L.
Trevathan, Miss Jean Carolyn
Tuggle, Aubrey
Tuggle, Gordon
Turner, Dr. Larry
Turner, Mrs. Larry
Tyler, Mrs. Runyon
Tyler, Runyon, Jr.
Tyren, Theodore T.
Tyren, Mrs. Theodore T.
Umstead, Percy W.
Umstead, Mrs. Percy W.
Umstead, Allan
Underwood, Dr. J. T.
Underwood, Mrs. J. T.
Underwood, J. T., Jr.
Underwood, Jack Dean
Underwood, Mrs. Jack Dean
Urquhart, Mrs. Lillian
Uzzle, D. W.
Uzzle, Mrs. D. W.
Uzzle, Dalma Wilson, Jr.
Uzzle, Granville Lipscomb
van Straaten, Harry J.
van Straaten, Mrs. Harry J.
Vinson, Jacqueline
Wade, Wallace
Wade, Wallace, Jr.
Wade, Mrs. Wallace, Jr.
Wadsworth, Dr. Joseph A. C.
Waite, Miss Lucille
Waite, Miss Nina
Waite, Miss Margaret
Walker, Mrs. C. E.
Walker, Dr. Marvin E.
Walker, Mrs. Marvin E.
Wall, Doris E.
Walters, A. H.
Walters, Mrs. A. H.
Ward, Charles E.
Ward, Mrs. Charles E.
Ward, Lochlin M.
Ward, Mrs. Lochlin M.
Warner, Mrs. G. Frank
Warren, George A.
Warren, Mrs. George A.

Warren, George A., Jr.
Warren, Gordon
Warren, Mrs. Gordon
Warren, W. F.
Warren, Mrs. W. F.
Warren, Miss Nancy
Warren, William Franklin, Jr.
Watkins, Mrs. N. S.
Watson, Miss Margaret Pauline
Weir, Harry M.
Weir, Mrs. Harry M.
Wolfling, Mrs. Welden
West, Mrs. A. T.
White, Finley T.
White, Mrs. Finley T.
White, Gilbert C.
White, Mrs. Gilbert C.
Wicker, Mrs. C. A.
Wilkerson, Joseph
Wilkinson, Mrs. Albert
Wilkinson, Albert G.
Wilkinson, Fred B.
Wilkinson, H. E., Jr.
Wilkinson, Mrs. H. E., Jr.
Wilkinson, Thomas N.
Wilkinson, Mrs. Thomas N.
Wilkinson, Thomas G.
Willets, Mrs. Charles A.
Williams, C. E.
Williams, Mrs. C. E.
Williams, J. Edgar
Williams, D. M.
Williams, Mrs. D. M.
Williams, Miss St. Clair
Williams, Miss Priscilla
Williams, Dan
Williams, Miss Etta
Williams, F. J.
Williams, Mrs. F. J.
Williams, F. J., Jr.
Wilson, C. T.
Wilson, Mrs. C. T.
Wilson, Dr. F. E.
Wilson, Miss Aileen
Wilson, Dr. Robert R.
Wilson, Mrs. Robert R.
Wily, Eugene M.
Wily, Mrs. Eugene M.
Wily, J. F., Jr.
Wily, Mrs. J. F., Jr.
Winder, Thomas A.
Winder, Mrs. Thomas A.
Windham, Miss Faye
Wood, Mrs. Wm. H.
Woods, Dr. James W.
Woods, Mrs. James W.
Wooten, James H., Jr.
Workman, Mrs. H. S.
Worth, Thomas C.
Worth, Mrs. Thomas C.
Worth, Miss Betty
Worth, Mrs. A. H.
Wright, Richard H., Jr.
Wright, Mrs. R. H., Jr.
Wright, Miss Turissa
Wright, Miss Elizabeth Scanlon
Wright, Miss Mary Elizabeth
Wynne, George V.
Wynne, Mrs. George V.
Wynne, Willis Holland
Wynne, Mrs. Willis Holland
Young, Miss Zoe

Joe Buchanan
Betsy Deichmann
Buckie Dunn
Jerry Elliott
Dick Hendrickson
Virginia Jackson
Julia Jones
Billy Maughan
Vernon Pratt
Bobby Rankin
Carol Robert
Ronald Rodenhizer
Betsy Scanlon
Dinny White
Sylvia Wilkinson
Geofrey Ward

Junior Department

Fourth Grade

Deanna Bradley
Janice Everett
Mary Elizabeth Gray
Margaret Hamblen
Jackie Holt
June Humphries
Wier Irvine
Carolyn Leary
Dorothy McDevett
Lynn Moorhead
Nancy Patton
Carl West
John F. Wily, Jr.

Fifth Grade

Lucius Bigelow
Ann Davis
Bill Gray
Sue Gray
Bill Murphy
Jacqueline Miller
Angeline Norris
Terry Odom
Frances Owen
Sandra Perry
John Pratt
Chas. Ross
Jimmy Tyler
Thos. White
Nancy Gay Lyon
Hope Smith

Sixth Grade

Mary Bigelow
Bill Couch, Jr.
Ann Creadick
Mary Dann
Susan Deichmann
Thomas Harris
Marian Hays
Muriel Hendrix
Carter Jones
Harriett Pickett
Dorothy Battle Rankin
M. de Bernieres Roberson, Jr.
Robert R. Wilson, Jr. (Chip)
Willa Conant

Junior High

Seventh Grade Boys

David Currie
Ronald Everett
Jan Oosting
Macon Patton
David Scanlon III
John Noel Simpson
Allan Umstead
Thomas Wilkinson

Eighth and Ninth Grade Boys

Charles Bartholomew
Al Bryant
Charles Carr
Charles A. Dukes, Jr.
Richard Dunn
Ralph Graham
Duncan Hays
Thomas Lee
Wendy Ligon
Richard Odom
Jon W. Regen
Frank Robert
David Rogers
Robert Ross
John Stinespring
Runyon Tyler
Granville Uzzle

Eighth and Ninth Grade Girls

Carolyn Beasley
Linda Conant
Elizabeth Davis
Gretchen Deichmann
Joan Earle
Sally Gray
Melba Lindsey
Joanne McDevett
Claudia Peeler
Rosemary Rhine
Patricia Stansbury
Gabrielle Stocker

Senior High School

Max Barnhardt
Hal Bowden
Jack Bowden
Jane Bolmeier
Joan Bolmeier
Harry Branch, Jr.
Norman Conant
Sylvia Conant
June Carr
Bobby Fuquay
Nancy Green
Agnes Hamblen
Ransome Harris
Laura Hays
Frances Jeffreys
David Jones
Fuller Karriker
Phillip Lewis
Lonnie T. Matthews, Jr.
James Odom
Sarah Anne Reese
Natalie Simpson
Victor Sydnor
Dan Uzzle
Fuller Whitaker

Young Adults

Mr. and Mrs. Bill Archie
Mr. and Mrs. George Arms
Mr. and Mrs. William Albright
Mr. and Mrs. D. L. Boone
Mrs. E. T. Buchanan, Jr.
Mr. Robert E. Chambers
Dr. and Mrs. Norman Conant
Mr. and Mrs. Roy Crenshaw
Mr. and Mrs. Isadore Croft
Dr. and Mrs. John Cuttino
Mrs. S. V. Daniel, Jr.
Mr. and Mrs. Laurence Fowler
Mrs. Charles Gomer
Mr. and Mrs. Balford Hackney
Mr. and Mrs. Bart Hagerty
Mr. and Mrs. Thomas Hay
Dr. and Mrs. Arden Howell
Mr. and Mrs. Tom Jones
Mr. and Mrs. John McArthur

Mrs. J. L. Sterling
Mrs. Wilma Stuart
Dr. and Mrs. H. L. Sirmans
Mr. Ted Tyren
Dr. and Mrs. Marvin Walker
Mr. and Mrs. Lochlin Ward
Mrs. A. T. West
Mrs. Willis Wynne

Business Women

Miss Julia Albright
Mrs. Joe A. Albright
Miss Jewel Bennett
Mrs. C. E. Bennett
Mrs. Hubert Brown
Mrs. Harry Christian
Mrs. G. T. Dunn
Mrs. Sadie Gallyon
Mrs. Clarice Gattis
Mrs. Rachel Greene
Mrs. C. E. Hooker
Miss Liza Jones
Mrs. J. A. Ligon
Mrs. F. K. Lindsey
Mrs. Hazel Myers
Miss Clara Murray
Mrs. W. S. McDevett
Miss Gladys Paulson
Mrs. Aline Rodenhizer
Mrs. Riley Reese
Dr. Annie T. Smith
Miss Ema Tholen
Mrs. J. L. Trevathan
Mrs. Eva Warren
Miss Lucille Waite
Miss Nina Waite
Mrs. N. S. Watkins
Mrs. H. S. Whitaker
Miss Zoe Young

Blacknall Bible Class

Mrs. H. E. Adams
Mrs. T. H. Antrim
Mrs. D. L. Boone
Mrs. R. H. Buckingham
Mrs. J. W. Carpenter
Mrs. Lena Champion
Mrs. Rodney Chase
Mrs. Eva Coley
Miss Annie H. Collins
Mrs. W. D. Croom
Mrs. Edith Davis
Mrs. Charles Dukes
Mrs. B. W. Elliott
Mrs. R. O. Everett
Mrs. A. L. Ferguson
Mrs. D. L. Garrard
Mrs. Lee Roy Gattis
Mrs. G. C. Glymph
Mrs. Lee Goodwin
Mrs. J. H. Gregory
Mrs. K. S. Grimson
Mrs. H. O. Gurganus
Mrs. W. A. Honeycutt
Mrs. Sallie Hammett
Mrs. Spears Hicks
Mrs. J. F. Hill
Mrs. J. R. Hopkins
Mrs. D. J. Huckabee
Mrs. W. B. Jeffreys
Mrs. T. R. Karriker
Mrs. R. N. Kemp
Mrs. T. C. Kerns
Mrs. C. F. Korstian
Mrs. J. B. Leathers
Mrs. J. Grover Lee
Mrs. P. C. Lewis
Mrs. D. L. McDonald
Mrs. Anna McGranahan
Mrs. L. T. Matthews
Mrs. E. C. Murray
Mrs. W. G. Murray

Mrs. W. L. Simpson
Mrs. W. L. Simpson
Mrs. W. W. Skinner
Mrs. W. I. Smith
Mrs. Gertrude A. Stow
Mrs. R. N. Strayhorn
Mrs. A. B. Taylor
Mrs. J. R. Tisdale
Mrs. George Warren
Mrs. Albert Wilkinson
Mrs. Fred Williams
Mrs. D. M. Williams
Mrs. T. A. Winder
Mrs. A. H. Worth
Mrs. R. R. Wilson
Mrs. George V. Wynne

Big Brothers' Bible Class

J. A. Albright
George Arms
T. H. Antrim
A. H. Baker
E. W. Beasley
H. W. Branch, Sr.
H. W. Branch, Jr.
S. O. Cates
R. Y. Chase
H. L. Christian
J. W. Christian
L. V. Craig
C. A. Croft
W. D. Croom
C. A. Dukes
B. W. Elliott
Coy M. Franklin
Lee Roy Gattis
John H. Gibson
G. C. Glymph
Lee C. Goodwin
Horace Hendrickson
C. S. Hicks
J. F. Hill
Thad C. Hill
W. B. Hinshaw
Tim A. Hudson
C. O. Huffer
J. E. Hulse
J. C. Hundley
R. G. Jones
J. B. Leathers
J. Grover Lee
L. C. Mann
L. T. Matthews, Sr.
J. M. McCaskill
D. L. McDonald
L. P. Miller
W. G. Murray
R. G. Montgomery
H. E. Montsinger, Jr.
B. B. Myers
J. A. Odom
R. D. Patterson
J. R. Patton
J. L. Pleasants
R. S. Rankin
J. M. Ray
Z. A. Rochelle
W. H. Simpson
W. L. Simpson
H. L. Sirmans
G. M. Spicer
J. W. Stone, Sr.
L. D. Styron
C. S. Sydnor
J. L. Trevathan
A. H. Walters
E. Gordon Warren
George A. Warren
W. Frank Warren
H. S. Whitaker
H. E. Wilkinson, Jr.
T. N. Wilkinson
A. G. Wilkinson

Lightning Source UK Ltd.
Milton Keynes UK
UKHW020022181218
334174UK00013B/2119/P